TOWNS AND CITIES

by

Joanna Brundle

©2017
Book Life
King's Lynn
Norfolk PE30 4LS

ISBN: 978-1-78637-047-1

Written by:
Joanna Brundle

Edited by:
Grace Jones

Designed by:
Matt Rumbelow

TOWNS AND CITIES

Contents

Look for the words in **bold** in the Glossary on page 23.

YOUR **LOCAL** AREA

What are **Towns** and **Cities**?

Towns and cities are **urban settlements**. Towns are bigger than villages but they are smaller than cities, in both area and **population**. Cities often have universities or important places of worship, like cathedrals.

This view of Moscow, Russia shows the bright lights of the city centre from above.

Cathedral of Brasília, Brazil

A capital city is often the most important city in a country and it is where the **government** is usually based. More than half of the world's population live in urban places. Megacities have ten million or more people living in them.

Every Australian state has a capital city. This is Sydney, the capital city of New South Wales.

New York City was the world's first megacity.

Where and Why?

Settlements began in places where the basic needs of people were met. Humans and their animals need water, so many towns and cities were built near rivers.

The city of Lanzhou, China stands on the Yellow River, one of the longest rivers in the world.

The soil around rivers and other sources of fresh water are usually rich in **nutrients** and good for growing crops.

Crops growing by the Mekong River in Laos

Towns and cities often grow in terms of their area, wealth and population because of the **natural resources** in an area, like coal or gold.

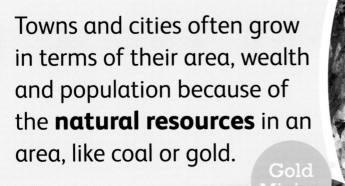

Gold Mining

The discovery of diamonds and gold brought people to Johannesburg, which has since become the biggest city in South Africa.

Sydney Harbour is one of the largest natural harbours in the world.

Many towns and cities have **ports** that have grown up around natural **harbours** where the water is deep enough for large boats to dock.

Towns and Cities in the Past

To keep people safer, so many towns and cities were built near water or on hills, which gave a good view of any approaching enemies.

The city of Rome, Italy is built on seven hills. The River Tiber also runs through it.

Edinburgh Castle, Scotland

Many old towns and cities have castles which were built to protect against **invaders**.

Nowadays, most castles only attract tourists!

Long ago, most people made their living by farming. In the UK, some settlements had the right, normally given by the king or queen, to hold markets for selling animals and crops. These became known as market towns. Even now, they still have a market square and sometimes a market cross.

Bakewell Market, England

A market cross, like this one in Salisbury, England was built to ask for God's blessing on the trade.

Buildings and Landmarks

Towns and cities usually have a town or city hall, with offices for the people in charge of the town or city. There are other offices for businesses, as well as places of worship, shops, hotels, restaurants, entertainment venues, like theatres, and sports arenas.

Church

Shops

City Hall, San Francisco, USA

Many towns and cities are known for particular buildings or landmarks, for example the Taj Mahal in Agra, India and St Basil's Cathedral in Moscow, Russia. Important events may be held at these buildings, which sometimes attract thousands of visitors.

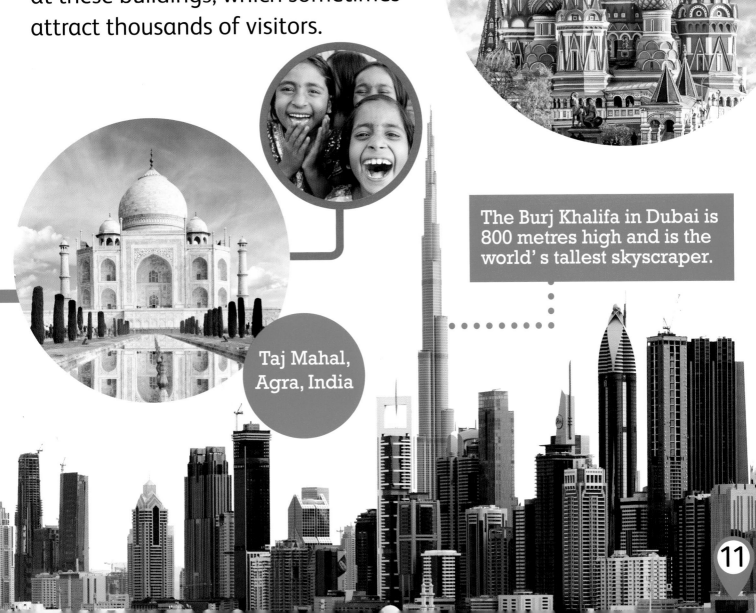

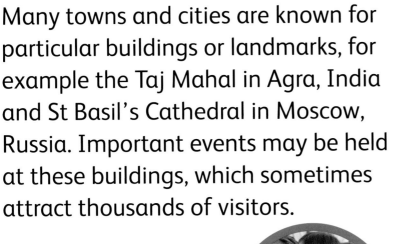

St. Basil's Cathedral, Moscow, Russia

Taj Mahal, Agra, India

The Burj Khalifa in Dubai is 800 metres high and is the world's tallest skyscraper.

Getting Around in **Towns** and **Cities**

There are often many different ways to get around a town or a city, including taking the train, catching the bus, jumping in a taxi, driving a car or riding a motorcycle. Many cities also have an airport and an underground railway system, sometimes called a metro or subway. Some even have a tram system.

Street tram, Helsinki, Finland

There are no traffic jams on the Shanghai Metro, China.

In India these rickshaw taxis dart in and out of the traffic.

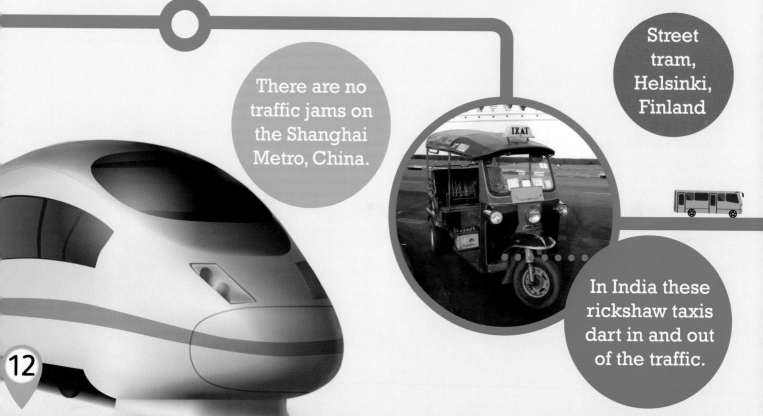

Commuters are people who live in towns outside the city centre, called suburbs, and travel into the city to work. It can be difficult to get around in busy city centres because of traffic **congestion**.

Transport for London

Congestion charging

Some cities try to reduce the number of cars on the roads by charging people who drive into the city centre.

Traffic congestion in China

Who Works in
Towns and Cities?

Towns and cities provide jobs in public services, such as in schools, hospitals and the police force. Shops, cafés, supermarkets and theatres all need people to run them. **Industries** need workers with special skills, like engineers to design and build cars.

Engineers building cars in Japan

Jobs in the United Kingdom

Public Services	5.7 Million
Retail (Shops)	2.8 Million
Manufacturing (Making Things)	2.6 Million

Some cities are known for particular kinds of jobs. Los Angeles, USA provides many jobs in the film industry. London, England and New York, USA provide many jobs in banking. Towns and cities all over India are now known for information technology jobs.

Film Industry in Los Angeles

Wall Street is home to the New York Stock Exchange and many banks.

Living in **Towns** and **Cities**

People choose to live in towns and cities because they provide good transport, jobs and lots of things to do. In towns, people mostly live in apartments or houses. Many houses have private gardens. In city centres, many people live in tower blocks with no gardens.

People are tightly packed into these tower blocks in Hong Kong.

A city park in Melbourne, Australia.

City living can be difficult and dangerous. Housing is expensive and sometimes there is not enough to go around. Even in rich countries, many people live on the streets or in **slums** inside shelters that they have made from cardboard and other materials.

Slums in Soweto, South Africa

A mask protects this cyclist from air **pollution** which is a big problem in Beijing, China.

What is There to Do in **Towns** and **Cities**?

Towns and cities are full of fun things to do. Many towns have a small theatre and a sports ground, but cities often have large concert halls and arenas that host international stars and major sporting competitions, like the football World Cup.

Olympic Stadium, London, England

Milan Opera House, Italy

In your local area, you can probably visit a library, a cinema, a museum and a swimming pool. Try drawing a simple map, like this one below, to show how you would walk between them. Remember to label the street names.

HIGH STREET

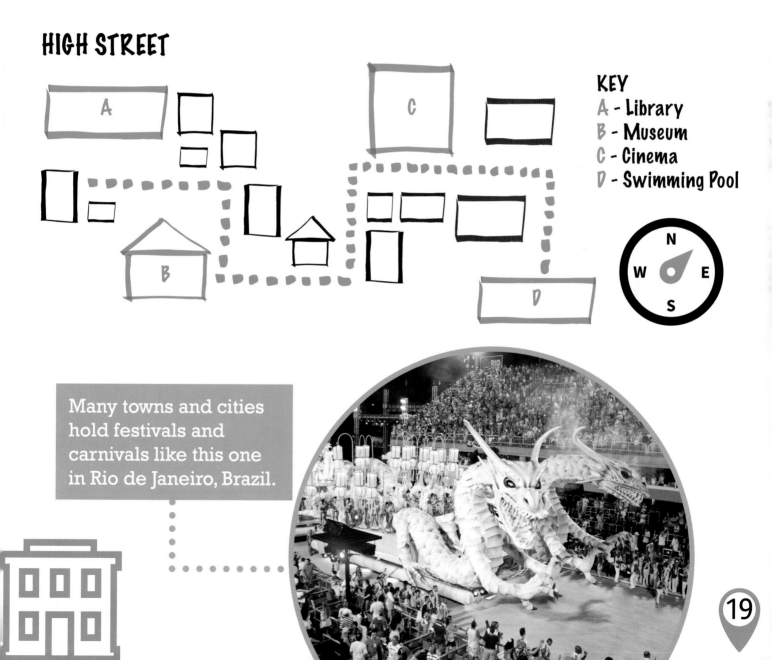

KEY
A - Library
B - Museum
C - Cinema
D - Swimming Pool

Many towns and cities hold festivals and carnivals like this one in Rio de Janeiro, Brazil.

Towns and Cities in the Future

Scientists think that by 2050, three quarters of people will live in an urban settlement. Because of this, it is important that towns and cities in the future are designed to produce less pollution and do less damage to the environment. Eco-towns and sustainable cities are settlements that recycle waste water and use power sources that do not run out, like solar power from the sun.

A solar panel plant in Shanghai, China.

Some cities, like Gothenburg, Sweden have bikes for hire, so you don't need a car.

Many more houses will be needed in the future because of the world's growing population. Town and city planners are planning for homes that people can afford to buy, which use green energy. Land that was once used for factories, known as brownfield sites, will be made available for new homes.

Brownfield Sites

New homes being built.

What's in a **Name**?

Some towns and cities are named after famous people.

Darwin, Australia is named after the scientist Charles Darwin.

Norwich, England

Some names, like Wells-next-the-Sea, reflect reflect the natural features of a place.. Place names also include old words – Norwich is made up of "nor" meaning north and "wic" meaning a collection of buildings.

This town in Wales has the longest place name in Europe. Try saying it!

LLANFAIRPWLLGWYNGYLLGOGERYCHWYRNDROBWLLLLANTYSILIOGOGOGOCH

Llan-vire-pooll-guin-gill-go-ger-u-queern-drob-ooll-llandus-ilio-gogo-goch

ARRIVA

Arriva Trains Wales / Trenau Arriva Cymru

Glossary

congestion	when there is too much traffic and cars cannot move freely
government	a group of people who are in charge of running a country
harbours	places where boats and ships can be moored
industries	businesses involved in producing goods for sale
invaders	people who enter and attack a place to try in order to take it over
natural resources	things which are of value and are created by natural processes rather than by humans
nutrients	naturally occurring substances that are needed for plants to grow
pollution	when something is added to the environment that is harmful to living things
population	the number of people living somewhere
ports	harbours that are used for trading , where ships can be loaded and unloaded
settlement	somewhere people live permanently, like a town or village
slums	dirty, overcrowded places where very poor people live
urban	to do with a town or city

Index

Photo Credits

Photocredits: Abbreviations: l-left, r-right, b-bottom, t-top, c-centre, m-middle.
Front Cover and 1: tl – iordani; bl – pisaphotography; cm – dibrova, tr – gorillaimages. 2 – pisaphotography, 3: tr – iordani; b – gorillaimages. 4: bl - Art Konovalov; br – gary yim. 5: l - Monkey Business Images; c - Joshua Haviv, tr – structuresxx. 6: m - Maksym Deliyergiyev; b - Banana Republic images. 7: tr – Ttstudio. tr inset - Joe Belanger. 7br – pisaphotography. 8: bl - Tetiana Dickens. tr – r.nagy. 9: bl – Walencienne. tr - Oscar Johns. 10: bl - Boris Stroujko, mr – jabiru. 11: tr – Reidl. Mc - Tukaram Karve, ml – Waj, b – alex7370. 12T - Nikiforov Alexander. 12 br – Yojik. 13: tr – Bikeworldtravel. br – chungking. 14 - Praphan Jampala. 15: tr – Javen, b – Kues. 16: t – leungchopan, bl - e X p o s e. 17: bl – testing. tr - Brian S. 18: bl - Sergey Nivens. mr - Rob Wilson. 19 br – Migel. 20: tr - Rolf_52, bl - gui jun peng. 21: tr - Mr Doomits; bl – mirrormere; bl inset – PathomP. 22: tl – fritz16; mr - Helen Hotson; b - Jane McIlroy. Images are courtesy of Shutterstock.com. With thanks to Getty Images, Thinkstock Photo and iStockphoto.